T0328512

SECRET KEEPER

SECRET KEEPER

Kerry Hammerton

Publication © Modjaji Books 2018

Text © Kerry Hammerton 2018
First published in 2018 by Modjaji Books
modjajibooks.co.za
ISBN 978-1-928215-57-8
e-book ISBN 978-1-928215-58-5
Book and cover design: Megan Ross
Cover artwork: Tammy Griffin

Set in Crimson Text

For Dad

Contents

1.

Dust

I am shopping in the supermarket
when the lights go off. The generator kicks in
but only a few lights come back on.
It's now dusk inside but I go on
shopping, what else can I do?
It's nicer because it is dimmer –
it isn't warmer or more comforting
but everything is no longer bright, the white
and neon packets aren't shouting in my face.
I can't read the ingredients on labels
unless I stand with my nose pressed
close to the shelves. My skin smells like dust,
as if I have driven a thousand miles
on a desert road. But it is not my skin
that smells like dust. It is the air around me.

Hungering for Darkness

A voice snatches me back
from the dark-edge of sleep –
my mouth slack with the effort
of burrowing away from the light.

I wander through half-lit rooms,
squint through curtain-gaps,
listen for something that isn't there.
The night air cools my sweated skin.

Back in my cold bed
I clutch the edge of a pillow,
the heavy torpedo of my body
hungering for darkness.

A Personal Winter

Early morning
an unblemished sky
and everywhere
the light is breaking. Yet
my mind has charged
into late evening,
shrouded stars,
wipers flinging rain
from my windscreen –
nothing ahead
but brake lights
flash / flash red.

unfamiliar landscape

snow is falling –
it settles into
drifts – forms
cold hollows –
enough to blur
the landscape

i am ignorant
of this geography –
perhaps the trees
can teach me
to stand still
under the weight of snow

Days like These

I wake up with tears
on my face,
salt-rims spreading
on my pillow.

I've come to expect this
on nights I dream of you,
your severed body

twenty-nine stab wounds
blood in the car.
And afterwards the rain.

Days like these
the clogged thickness
of everything
weighs me down.

as the walls sway

outside a full moon beckons
she watches
the billowing fog
shadows swelling

under trees
overhead branches creak
like ghostly bones

rain pools
on the verandah
a phantom oar dips
and splashes

she remembers
from her life
the upright spines
of books
the red
in that autumn dress

her gaze fastens
on the polished floor
as the walls sway
under this sickness
    this wanting
to open the door

to visitors
who aren't there

Divers

The boat's engine no longer thuds *A flutter of panic*
it can't come any closer *takes nest in the back of my throat.*
the waves are too rough, too high. I can see it *In my legs, my lower back*
cresting on a swell and disappearing, *I find muscles and grit*
cresting and disappearing. *my arms rotating through the water.*
A flag is up: divers in the water. *Clouds are menacing rain,*
The sea is murky, *a distant boom of thunder.*
our bodies shoved and threatened *And then my strength is sucked out*
by currents and shadows. Arms wearied, *by the drowning ocean,*
shoulders weighed down, *a wave breaks over my head.*
salt burning my eyes *Body hanging useless in the water*
saltwater filling my mouth, *countermanding the distress*
I feel dragged backwards, *signals in my brain.*
rammed and battered. *The flutter moves to my chest,*
I look up, *waves break across my face,*
the boat is still far away. *tears stinging my eyes,*
I can't see anyone else *breath sharp and ragged, the light*
in the water. *threatens to close above my head.*

All I Want

The moon hangs on the horizon
too heavy to lift its head
above the trees.

He stands on top of the hill –
breathfrostedgreycoated –
holds my gaze,

paces to test my obedience.
There is an answering surge
from beneath my breast.

Once he has claimed his territory
he lifts his head and howls.
Released I turn away

when all I want to do is run
long-legged and fierce
through the snow

expose my throat to his teeth –
to tear and choke –
staining my neck red.

Her

If I pass a mirror, I turn away,
I do not want to look at her
and she does not want to be seen. Sometimes
I'm not quick enough and catch
a glimpse of the veined arch
of her foot. When I hold up
my breasts as I step out of the bath
she seems to gawk at the knotted joints
in my feet, age-flecked hands, sagging
elbows, softening pudenda.
I think she must count each new grey hair.
I want to ask her what it's like to not
care, I want to know her intimate life,
the men she wants, the ones I don't.
I search along the seams of our life
to find the tear, the tearing
apart, maybe I didn't love her enough,
maybe I'll never love her enough.
At half night when the mirror is dark
I can gaze at the faded sea-blue
of my eyes and it's then
I'm sure I can see her
not looking at me.

Exhibit

I am no longer myself,
some slippage

has occurred – the silences
and viscera of my body sliding,

skin softening. I get tired.
Too many sleepless nights.

I want to look back and say
there was only love

but in the museum of life
my body and I

would be in different rooms –
between us

hooks of anger and hurt
pulled tight through skin and heart.

water rising

                              wind
                    today
         (trees skeletal
              horizontal)

              rain
         yesterday more
    (street lamps
         tilted)

                    (buildings concealed)
              across the land
                    mist

         fog
    settling
    (stars blank)

                              expected
    (people injured
         dying)
                    hail

         on sunday
    (earth washed away)
         sleet

                    snow
                    forecast
    (clouds grey)

                    snow
      forecast
      (sky black)

(water rising)

A Conversation with Nina Cassian

What is it like to be •ea•? I ask
'I no longer notice my ugly hea•'
she says *'an• squirrels live*
in my green be•room. The sun shines
at night. I write poetry
all •ay' And then she laughs,
that unmistakable head thrown back,
and lights a cigarette. What
I really want to know: how she wrote
after losing everything: furniture,
mementos, notebooks, home,
country, language. *'I learnt*
to listen to footsteps while
hanging over a cliff. I close•
a season behin• me an• I swam out far.'

Things I Keep from My Mother

When I lost my virginity, who with;
how that nice boy, the one she liked,
wasn't nice behind closed doors; and other things
I couldn't even tell my friends.

When I look at my hands
I see her ageing hands. Her drawn-in lips
remind me of her mother's aged lips –
but these are things I do not tell her.

There is much my mother doesn't know –
how many lovers I've had;
why I live so far away from home;
how often despair rises in me.

More than Half

I've lived more than half my life.
More than half. Now a constraining sleeplessness
threatens me at night. No more 'long-haul'
for me, no more 'let's see if this works out'.
Today there was no rain. Pigeons cooed
and mate-danced in the summer heat.
I went to work. I came home.
I didn't fall in love. The sky was clear.
The traffic light. The wind was a fresh breeze.
I probably met my soul-mate
on a day like this and
let him go.

2.

'And then the angels revealed themselves to me…as irresistible forces of the spirit, malleable to the most turbid and secret states of my nature. I unleashed them in bands, as blind reincarnations of all the cruelty, desolation, agony, terror and occasional good that was within me and closed in on me.'

Rafael Alberti *Concerning the Angels* (1928)

The Horse Angel

of shod hoof and trotting gait
of long foreleg muscles
arrives to teach me

to stand-still
to bind with the herd

I take too long
hold on too tight

she stands on my feet
pulls in another direction

until she is herself
again cantering into
her own flight

The Sleepless Angel

My bedroom is stained
with the bitter smoke
from his cigarette.

I try and wait him out,
but he's done this before,
hunkered down

wings folded carefully.
When I am half-asleep
he will drip blood

from the ceiling; whisper
into my ears; trail feathers
across my face.

In this half-dream moment
I can smell the fearful
sweat of him,

his nicotined fingers,
the oily grime
under his nails.

The Carrion Angel

Rusted sword,
knotted hair,
blood-soaked feathers.

He smells like the end
of the world: sulphur
and festering sores.

He doesn't remember heaven
or the fall or why
other angels shun him.

He longs to be bloodied
teeth tearing through
dead and decaying flesh

His ears are tuned to
the whimpers and dying
cries of badger, fox,

muskrat, owl – the snap
of rodent traps.

The Dream Angels

They wait for a blackened moon
then sidle in –
infecting dreams with love

and lust, and flight.
I say prayers
but they come back

grimfaced, sharpening
halberds and swords
on stolen grindstones.

Their muddy boots mar
the kitchen floor; their bloodgutted kill
stinks in pots on the stove.

To keep me honeyed
they chant mellifluously
as if they were still in heaven.

The Dark Angel

He wants to be an angel
of snowless mountains or
the east winds

but his blackness shimmers.
Bowstring pulled taut
he always aims to kill.

Coldheart. Inward.
In him
accord is impossible.

Requiem

the crow of my mind
spreads sheeny black wings

beak tears through
the marrow of my spine

tongue throttled I
caw-caw

I am going mad again
light candles

let the incense smoulder
sing the mass;

remember to burn
my bones and flesh.

The Death Angel

The city mutes itself around me
sound by sound: jackhammers,
hooting cars, the shout of flower-sellers

until his breathing
is the only thing I hear.
His shadow has become

my shadow.
When I look at the night sky
I can't see the moon

only a black void
drifting
between the stars.

3.

And James

It was summer (it was hot).
It was some time in the 80s,
and I was almost seventeen.
The cousins were here. Not all the cousins just two.
Younger than us but seeming more sophisticated
introducing us to Soft Cell and The Human League.
They looked like me and my brother –
in a cousin sort of way
a shape of a nose, a fall of hair across a face.

The cousins and a house on the beach.
There it wasn't just us and the cousins (a brother and sister),
there were others. The girls slept
in a long bedroom on the side of the house
where the boys tried to spy on us.
Denise with the small tits.
I don't know why she was there.
And for a few days Jimmy and Allie
and Colleen and Debbie and Sean.
And Neville. Neville must have been there.
But maybe he wasn't – or that was a different summer.

James was there that summer for sure.
And if James was there then Philip was there. And Tim.
(Tim died in a motorbike accident years later. Jimmy's dead too.
Everyone else is still alive. Except my Dad, who's just died.
And Gwyneth my aunt – mother of the cousins).
The cousins with their English accents. And their music.
Laid back and louche,
smoking behind the library in the small seaside town,
cajoling us to play tennis in the humid heat.

The parents have faded with their
drinking too much, braaing in the back garden, yelling
at us, leaving us alone.
But James. Yes I remember James.
Sneaking away from the crowd with him.

That summer there were cousins.
We smoked. We played tennis.
We drove to the coast. There was a large house.
And James. And sex on the beach.

Forever Almost

They finally learnt to be rebels
in their thirties – fresh tattoos
and belly rings. She stayed an extra week
just to be part of the midnight talks,
the wine, the laughter around the table.
Long evening walks on the beach
to cool their feet,
sun-tanning on the balcony
and making promises to no-one.

She can never untangle each memory,
find the moment her son
was conceived: the house torn down now,
a nightclub in the cinema, the tidal
pool washed away by storms and
waves, the beach narrowed and
inaccessible. *I wante* it to go on
forever*, she thinks, *for us to be
forever almost grown-up.*

In Yesterday

It was yesterday. The last telephone call
when there was no longer an us
but only him there and me here his voice beseeching
come back. Before yesterday there were rows
of green beer bottles then no longer talking or listening
just bruised flesh and fists through the door.
No longer us. Just him there
and me here. Yesterday the last telephone call and a bullet
in the chamber and him.
His frantic voice begging me no bloody use
attached by lines of memory the holidays of sun
and how every night he ran me a bath and those
rows of beer bottles. His voice pleading
how did it end? That trigger chamber close
to his finger. Yet before yesterday
there was also tea in bed every morning and then
that bath at night and calling each other
Mr and Mrs Beebe. Then it was the twisted
mouth of him, the grimace in his belly,
the fists, the doors, the burns, the bruises, the shouting.
Then no longer us and yesterday
the chambered bullet. I am not there.
That triggered finger. Now I know it's not
the death-end how of him,
but in yesterday it tremored like the end.

i wish it was summer

you're laughing
        at something you're reading
i wish it was summer
        you half naked
i would have to abandon my chair
my book   this moment
disturb you

you'd make room for me on the floor
my nose sharpened by your sweat
    my fingers hurting
    wanting to unbutton your jeans
give way   to the loosening in my belly
i would have to listen to you read
        kiss you first
your hands buried in my hair
brush my fingers   across your chest
    across your back
nip an earlobe
your eyes widening
at this,
    this slow
    coming to it

We Walked Anyway

That morning. The mist. The mountains
and sea invisible. The streets
flooded with overnight rain. We walked
anyway. Lobelias and campanulas
showing off purple-blue. Ferns
bright green with new growth.
The hurry-rush of water over rocks
drowning anything we could have said.
I followed the familiar curve of your calf and knee.
Swartbas and Tree Fuchsias thin
and upright in the forest.
Buckled branches forming
a tree-cave at the end of a long uphill.
A peaty soaked-earth smell.
Red clay and slippery fallen leaf
mulch clinging to our boots.
The way down quieter
but we still had nothing to say.
You shook my hand in the parking lot.
Drove away. Left me in the coffee shop
ordering breakfast, trying to work out
how I could do this without you.

To Love

I wanted the stars then, and
the spaces between the stars.
I even wanted the moon.
I would have settled
for a sizzle of sparklers,
a familiar unshaven cheek
in the morning, lazy warm in bed
knees behind my knees.

But it is winter here again –
the sky is mottled grey
clouds have gathered
in every corner of this room
and I have become the place to which
you've lost your way.

Which Fantasy

She caresses the cleft
of her buttocks, the crease
behind her knees.

Her fingers trail from lips
down the edge of her throat
linger at the top of her breasts.

Which fantasy
should she play out tonight?
The virginal schoolgirl

who hesitates to touch
her own skin?
Or the on-display-for-a-camera

fingers that pinch nipples,
fingers that find
the heat of her clitoris?

Maybe a vibrator?
Yes, the purple one.
And the memory of

the two dark-haired brothers
their nipping teeth
and rough, rough hands.

Ambush

i let an octopus kiss me
head resting on my tongue
mouth gagged

salt water sliding
down my throat
i let an octopus slide between my legs

tentacled arms
puckered nipples
welts on my skin

beaked mouth engulfing
clitoris   labia   vagina
i felt the weight of the ocean howl

i let an octopus between my legs
i let his tentacles tear me open
pink swelling pulsing to blood red

Karaoke

Close your eyes. Remember
the bruiser you met
in the bar last night. His snake tattoo.
How he claimed you with his eyes.
When he inclined his head something
loosened inside. You were thinking
those dumb thoughts again. How
you'd have just one drink.
That you'd only say hello.
That you wouldn't kiss him
or let him put his hands
inside your shirt. Or fuck him
in the alley behind the bar.
The regulars watched you walk over
with steel in their eyes,
but no-one stopped you.
They knew they'd all be slurring karaoke
with you later, high on
the loneliness in your eyes.

Where it Starts

It cannot start with him
locking the door. Or his words.
It starts with the gift
of chocolates. A bottle of red wine.
Or maybe with the telephone call:
he's coming into town.
It doesn't start with the hard press
of his chest against my breasts,
his hands gripping my wrists.
It cannot start with a bed
that wasn't my own.
It doesn't start with his teeth
rough on my nipples.
It has to start with something far away –
me stumbling out of a smoky party,
and him leaning against a car on the street
talking on his phone.
He knew my name.
His words – *so we are alone*
finally. Then locking the door.
But we are not there yet.
We had lunch once.
Coffee a few times. Once
a walk on the mountain.
A gift of pens.
We had a drink at the party.
He knew my name.
He called to hear my voice,
once. Then he was coming into town
again. *It's a crow*, he said,
a house on the beach.

A weeken away. I said no.
He called again. Again. Again.
I went for one night.
It never happens to someone like me –
this dismantling of all refusals.
It could never have started on a Sunday
when everyone has gone home
or is asleep in the afternoon sun.
It could not start with a locked door
or *Alone finally.* I never said yes.

You Again

I had not thought about you
for months, years and now you stand
behind my right shoulder—
a pale ghost with long dark hair—
just out of the reach of my eye.
Always at night, sometimes
at dawn, and now even
when it is day. I want to
take an axe to my head,
cleave my skull,
gouge out that part of my brain
that holds onto you
and spits out these memories.

You were never anything like a ghost.
Could it be that you've died? And here
you are again, somewhere
you are not supposed to be.
I feel hollow in odd parts of my body
like my left ear, my right elbow
and the toe I broke before
I even knew you. I shake my head
you don't disappear.
So many poems I've written about you,
why should I write one more line?

No-one to Say

To upstage the dead is easy.
No-one to argue, to say *say something,*
anything. To push fists into pockets,
walls, doors. No-one to say sorry.
To go away. To comeback. No-one to say
this is right, this wrong. Not to say
not love. There was that. It was you.
The charm of you. Our dogs. The fists.
The shouting. The mountain holidays.
The walks. Sundowners. The love.
You were an ocean to cross to get to this.
This pen, paper, writing: *Death. Love. You.*

First Time

There was no blood. We fumbled,
a lot. It was 1981. It must have been
summer. Hot. Sticky. Bodies.
Elbows and shoulders and legs.

I remember your don't-fuck-with-me
18-year-old arrogance, your large
hands. You bullied me, I see that now.
Although it was my bravado
that begged you for sex.

The borrowed bed, the wooden
headboard, the sagging mattress,
the 1970s bedspread and sheets
smelling of another boy's semen
and sweat. You kept asking

is this alright for you?
I didn't really know what to say
felt stupid. Afterwards
I wanted to call myself a woman,
proclaim – if only to my diary –
I am a woman now.
But it didn't feel like that.

After that it was always
a borrowed bed or furtive
groping in my parents' lounge
after everyone else had gone to bed.

All I have is a key-ring
you made – my name
carved into perspex –
and a blurring photograph
of your face.

The Secret Keeper

They disturb my upper palate,
hover close to my throat, knock
against my teeth. Buzz and dart,
tickle the soft parts of my tongue.

They want me to open my mouth.
I press my upper lip down,
edge lips between teeth and bite
hard. Later I'll wrap my head

in gauze, gloved and booted, walk
through my garden, test the fullness
of my hives. When I find an empty
chamber I'll unwind the gauze

from my jaw and put my mouth
to the waxy comb. My lips will part
and the secrets escape. My reward?
a slur of honey across my lips.

I will have some respite. A few hours.
Maybe a night. If I'm is lucky – a few days.
The secrets always come back,
hairy bodies crammed into my mouth.

My garden is teeming with hives.

Days Shortening

To think I wasted all that time
trying to make sense of
the I-love-yous, the phonecalls
made, the ones that weren't.
Those hours spent thinking and wondering,
hours I'll never have back.
Not that anything will change,
but what if I had paid attention, just for once?
– and waited – with no what-ifs
or maybes or somehows or
tomorrows. With no possibility
of goodbye or even of hello.
I know what's waiting for me –
the storms of winter;
a lessening of desire; a burrowing
in; days shortening
to night.

4.

Dad

The short walk up the little hill from the beach
saps him.

I am the one who carries the umbrella
and the cooler-box, his chair
clutched under my arm.

His scapulae poke
through all the layers
he is wearing this summer:
vest, long sleeved cotton shirt, jersey.

It seems like yesterday I sat
on his shoulders, ready to do battle
in the swimming pool;
danced on magic stilts he cobbled together
from old paint cans and bits of string.

His dimming eyes settle on me now
for affirmation.

The Darkness of Grief

I imagine him already dead.
His funeral suit pooling
around shrunken arms
and legs.
He barely takes up the space
in his coffin.

His face jowled,
white hair still thick,
combed forward to cover
a receding hair-line.

I imagine jets of gas,
flames hissing
as they consume him.

I imagine later that night
those of us left behind
will dowse each other for memories
to fade the darkness of our grief,
and bicker
about where to scatter his ashes.

For Dad, Dying

You are far out now, light fading,
the edge of things gone.

We stand on the shore
sand firm under our feet.

We light candles – not to call you back
but to give you a flickering light to keep
behind you as you move further into darkness.

The seagulls have silenced
their squawking, stopped their fighting
and brawling. The dune grasses bend

their heads in the wind. Planes
have altered their flight paths
to create a sky that is open and free.

We will hold hands and hinder our tears
until you can no longer see us.

Let nostalgia go. Grant death to yourself.
Hurtle now. Let nothing hold you back.

This Year

March

Dad's lungs thickening
with disease – they won't

let me visit. Weeks later
his skull-face is unfamiliar.

Someone is teaching him how to
walk again, his shoes sandpaper-

rasp across the floor
When he falls it's easy

to pick him up, his bones
hollow like a bird's.

All he wants to do is sleep,
we nag him to keep on living.

June

The man selling key-rings
at the traffic lights knows

something is wrong,
asks if I am alright.

I shake my head –
not today, no thank you

not today.
Meaning not today,

I don't want a key-ring, not today –
but he knows what I really mean.

I look through my grief and wonder
how I will ever get to the other side.

September

Death hugs his face, drapes
across his shoulders, stiffens

his limbs, hardens his ears
shrouds him in thinness,

but death doesn't hug him
hard enough – it leaves room

for his hands to shake,
for his feet to trip and fall.

He is now something curved
and broken that wants to be straight,

his eyes turned away from us
watching the stars in his own sky.

December

The European cold
seeps into my thighs

bones so heavy
I can no longer hold

myself upright,
feet slipping on

winter rain
pooled on cobblestones.

The year has tumbled
towards its own end

his dying is finally over
we can begin mourning now.

The Last Day in Paris

All the time the world was rushing
me towards mourning
there was no sign of it.

It was raining – yes –
but the Seine didn't overflow.
The Metro rumbled and rolled us

to Saint-Merri church
and the piano music that
soared to the roof. Afterwards

the coffee was bitter and strong –
charmed waiters called me Madame.
Last day in Paris

the tears I spilled a few hours earlier
at a small harsh word from you
were just waiting

to find their full flood
at my brother's voice
'Dad died this afternoon'.

Arriving Home

I left winter behind
but summer showed up
            off-centre
leaves too green
        mountains too large
sun too bright
            or maybe
filtered too thickly
                through cloud
my car seat
        too close to the steering wheel
the flesh on my face
        peeled
            to the bone

My Other Life

I am better at my other life,
where no-one is dead,
where sadness doesn't press
its cold weight into my sternum
creep along my clavicle,
breathe into my spine.

Where my mother remembers
to wear matching shoes
and doesn't need someone to
hold her hand
while she looks for a will,
the deeds to the house.

Where we don't have to hear
condolences fall like heavy stones
into the dry well of our grief.
Where I don't feel my own mortality
at night: black sky, stars,
the milky way.

My Father's Watch

In my father's last fall
its face cracked
its body broke

I wanted my father's watch
I wanted the large hands and numbers
to tick me towards to my own death

I've inherited instead
his slowly greying hair.

Acknowledgements and Notes

My mother as always. Robert Berold who has an uncanny ability to see the truth of a poem. Thank you for your wisdom and listening to me. Finuala Dowling who provided the wine and light relief, and continued encouragement. My fellow MA students. Thank you for your insights and discussions and laughter, the poetry readings. I wish we had had more time together.

Some of the poems in this collection were previously published in the following South African literary journals: *New Coin*, *Stanza* and *New Contrast* and on-line in *Aero▸rome*, *Typecast* and *itch*.

the walls sway was written as an echo of Jorie Graham's poem "Vertigo". **water rising** follows the form of Federico García Lorca's poem "Song with a Particular Movement". **Divers in the Water** adapts a form invented by British poet Hannah Lowe. **All I Want** was inspired by Chavisa Woods' short story "The Bell Tower". **Her:** the first three lines are from the Sharon Olds' poem "Known to be Left". **Days Shortening** borrows the line 'I know what's waiting for me' from Nina Cassian's poem "Summer X-Rays". **A Conversation with Nina Cassian** is an imagined conversation with the Romanian poet. The ideas that are used in her speech are borrowed from her poems. **The Angel Poems** – these poems were influenced by Rafael Alberti's *Concerning the Angels*. Not the specific angels but the idea of writing about angels that are not angelic but from a place of despair. **In Yesterday and No-one to Say** were inspired by Noy Holland's short stories "Rooster. Pollard. Cricket. Goose" and "Orbit" and her use of idiosyncratic syntax and circular way of writing. **i wish it was summer** borrow directness, line lengths and indents from Lenore Kandel's collection *The Love Book.* **Ambush** was written in response to Penny Siopis' painting Ambush [2008], which is a response to Hokusai's woodcut, The Fisherman's Wife [1820]. **This Year: September** – the final lines in this poem use words and phrases from the final lines of Rafael Alberti's poem "The Grammar School Angels". **For Dad, Dying** – the last stanza borrows words and phrases from the last stanza in Rafael Alberti's poem "The Bull of Death".

Printed in the United States
By Bookmasters